# Carrots Don't Talk!

Written by Kathryn E. Lewis • Illustrated by JoAnn Kitchel

Silver Burdett Ginn
A Division of Simon & Schuster
160 Gould Street
Needham Heights, MA 02194 - 2310

Modern Curriculum Press
A Division of Simon & Schuster
299 Jefferson Road, P.O. Box 480
Parsippany, NJ 07054 - 0480

Design and production by BIG BLUE DOT

ISBN: 0-663-59389-1  Silver Burdett Ginn
ISBN: 08136-0933-0  Modern Curriculum Press

1 2 3 4 5 6 7 8 9 10 SP 01 00 99 98 97 96 95

Once long ago, a boy and
a girl were playing.

"I'm hungry," said the boy. "I don't have anything to eat."
"I have an apple," said the girl.

"I don't want an apple," said the boy.
"I think I'll go to the garden to get a carrot."
"I'll stay here," said the girl.

So the boy went to the garden. He began to pull on a carrot. Every time he pulled, he heard someone talking.

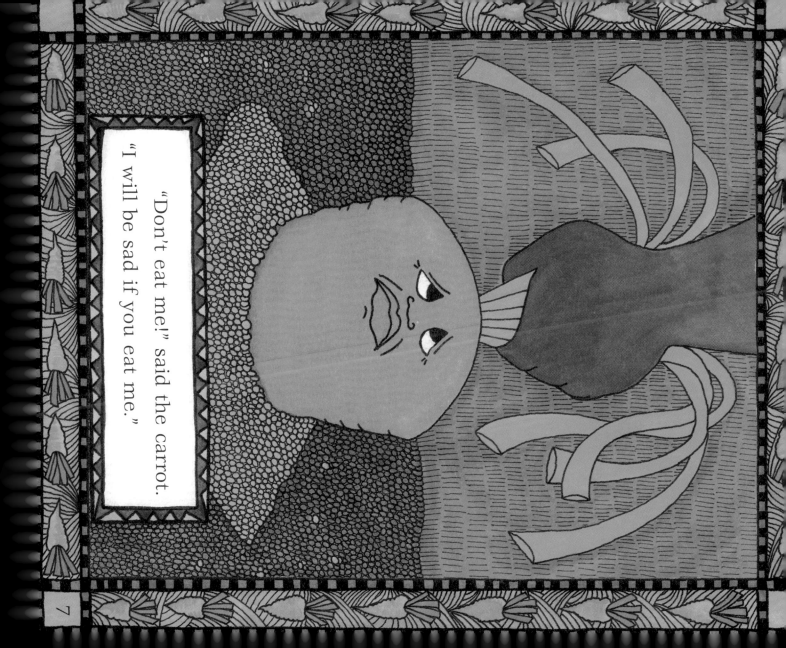

"Don't eat me!" said the carrot.
"I will be sad if you eat me."

The boy jumped up. He said, "It can't be the carrot. I am sure that carrots don't talk."

8

"Don't be so sure," said the dog, who was resting.

9

"What?" said the boy. "Now who is talking to me? Is someone here?"

"Yes," said the dog. "Someone is here. The carrot is here, and I am here."

The boy had never heard of a talking carrot or a talking dog. He was very scared. He ran behind the tree to hide.

13

"Don't hide here," said the tree.

The boy jumped back. He asked, "Is someone talking to me? It can't be the tree. I am sure that trees don't talk."

"Don't be so sure," said the tree. "What?" said the boy. "Is someone here?"

"Yes," said the tree. "The carrot is here. The dog is here, and I am here."

The boy had never heard of a talking carrot or a talking dog or a talking tree. He was very scared, so he ran to find the girl.

"Did you find anything to eat?" the girl asked.

"No," said the boy. "Every time I tried to pull out a carrot, the carrot talked to me. Then a dog talked to me, and then a tree talked to me!"

The girl gave the boy a sad look. "You have been out in the sun too long. You should go home and rest." "Yes, I do need a rest," said the boy.

As he walked away, the girl sat down to eat her apple.

"What a silly boy!" said the apple.
"Everyone knows that carrots don't talk."